RO SPORTS
UPERSTARS

SUPERSTARS OF THE DENVER BRONCOS

by M.K. Osborne

AMICUS | AMICUS INK

Library of Congress Cataloging-in-Publication Data
Names: Osborne, M. K., author.
Title: Superstars of the Denver Broncos / By M.K. Osborne.
Description: Mankato, MN : Amicus, [2019] |
Series: Pro sports superstars NFL | Includes index. | Audience: K to Grade 3.
Identifiers: LCCN 2017057178 (print) | LCCN 2018007110 (ebook) | ISBN 9781681514864 (pdf) | ISBN 9781681514048 (library binding) | ISBN 9781681523248 (pbk.)
Subjects: LCSH: Denver Broncos (Football team)--Biography--Juvenile literature. | Denver Broncos (Football team)--History--Juvenile literature. | Football players--United States--Biography--Juvenile literature.
Classification: LCC GV956.D37 (ebook) | LCC GV956.D37 O74 2019 (print) | DDC 796.332/640978883--dc23
LC record available at https://lccn.loc.gov/2017057178

Photo Credits: All photos from Associated Press except Getty Images/Doug Pensinger/Staff, 4-5; Newscom/Cliff Welch/Icon Sportswire 357/Cliff Welch/Icon Sportswire, 18–19

Series Designer: Veronica Scott
Designer: Ciara Beitlich/ Veronica Scott
Photo Researcher: Holly Young

Printed in China
HC 10 9 8 7 6 5 4 3 2 1
PB 10 9 8 7 6 5 4 3 2 1

TABLE OF CONTENTS

GET TO KNOW THE BRONCOS

The Denver Broncos have played in eight Super Bowls. They won three of them. They started in a league called the **AFL** in 1960. They joined the **NFL** in 1970.

Who are some of the Broncos' greatest stars? Let's find out!

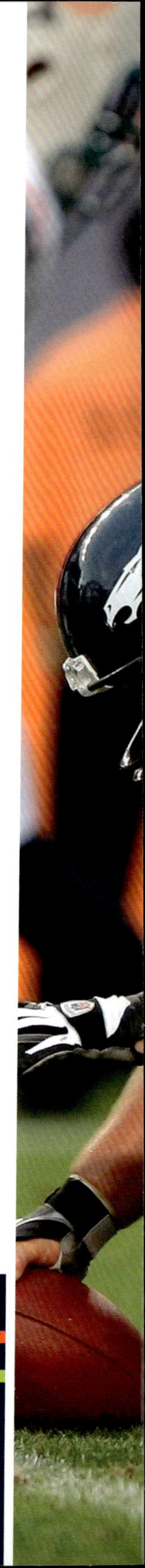

Little played for the Broncos for eight years. He scored 54 touchdowns.

FLOYD LITTLE

Floyd Little was a star runner. He was hard to tackle. In 1971, he won an award for **rushing**. He ran 1,133 yards in one season. Little went to three **Pro Bowls**. He was added to the NFL Hall of Fame in 2010.

JOHN ELWAY

John Elway had a great arm. He was a star **quarterback**. Elway led the Broncos to five Super Bowls. They won two of them. He was the Super Bowl **MVP** in 1998. He played for the Broncos for 16 seasons.

Elway was added to the NFL Hall of Fame in 2004.

Atwater played in seven straight Pro Bowls, from 1990 to 1996.

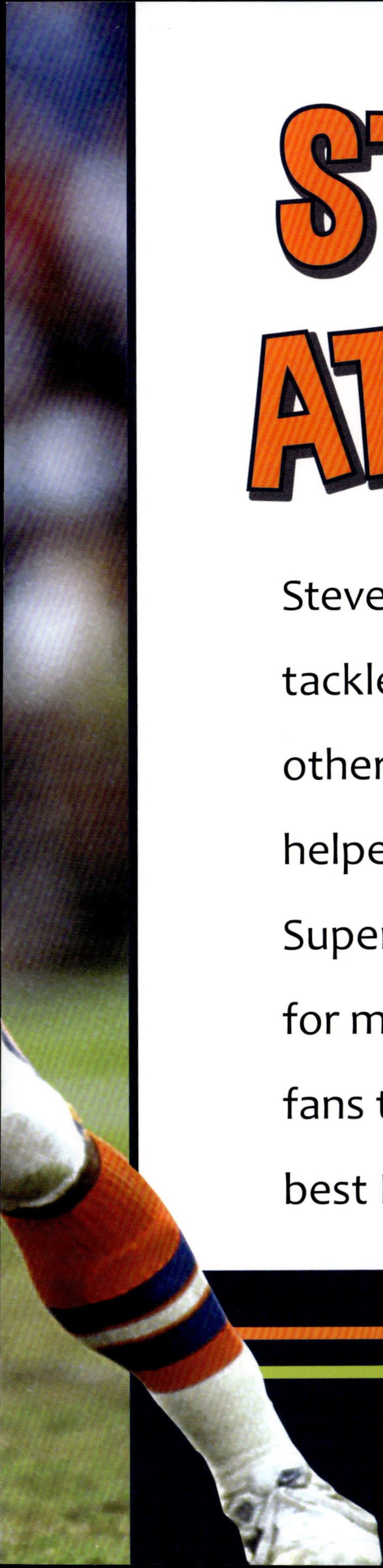

STEVE ATWATER

Steve Atwater was a good tackler. He often stopped the other team from scoring. He helped the Broncos win two Super Bowls. He was known for making big plays. Many fans think he is one of the best Broncos ever.

84
BRONCOS

SHANNON SHARPE

Shannon Sharpe was a great **tight end**. He was good at blocking. He could catch passes well. He helped the Broncos win two Super Bowls in a row, in 1998 and 1999.

TERRELL DAVIS

Terrell Davis was a running back. He was fast. He knew how to score. Davis only played four seasons with the Broncos. He helped the Broncos win back-to-back Super Bowls. He joined the NFL Hall of Fame in 2017.

Riddell
30

The Broncos picked Thomas in the first round of the 2010 NFL Draft.

DEMARYIUS THOMAS

Demaryius Thomas plays **offense**. Thomas is big. He is strong. But he is also fast. He set a Broncos record in 2014. He gained 100 yards in ten games during the season. Thomas has been to five Pro Bowls.

VON MILLER

Von Miller plays **defense**. He loves to sack the quarterback. He joined the Broncos in 2011. Not only is he strong, but he is fast, too. He helped the Broncos win a Super Bowl in 2016.

Miller was named MVP of the 2016 Super Bowl.

RAIDERS
BRONCOS
56
BRONCOS
56

YOUNG STAR

Shane Ray is an outside linebacker. He started playing for the Broncos in 2014. He is good at sacking. He made 68 tackles in his first 30 games. Ray is a great defensive player.

Let's watch and see who will be the next star of the Broncos!

TEAM FAST FACTS

Founded: 1960

Home Stadium: Sports Authority Field at Mile High (Denver, Colorado)

Super Bowl Titles: 3
(1998, 1999 and 2016)

Nicknames: Orange Crush

Hall of Fame Players: 8
including Floyd Little, John Elway, Shannon Sharpe, and Terrell Davis

WORDS TO KNOW

AFL – the American Football League; a league that played in the 1960s

defense – the group of players that tries to stop the other team from scoring

MVP – Most Valuable Player; an honor given to the best player each season

NFL – National Football League; a group that organizes and promotes pro football games

offense – the group of players that tries to score

Pro Bowl – the NFL's all-star game

quarterback – a player whose main jobs are to lead the offense and throw passes

rushing – running with the ball

tight end – a player whose main jobs are to catch passes and block

LEARN MORE

Books

Buckley Jr., James. *Von Miller and the Denver Broncos: Super Bowl 50*. New York: Bearport Publishing Company, Inc., 2017.

Morey, Allan. *The Denver Broncos Story*. Minneapolis: Bellwether Media, Inc., 2017.

Websites

Denver Broncos—Official Site
http://www.denverbroncos.com/
Watch video clips and view photos of the Denver Broncos.

NFL.com
http://nfl.com
Check out pictures and your favorite football players' stats.

NFL Rush
http://www.nflrush.com
Play games and learn how to be a part of NFL PLAY 60.

Every effort has been made to ensure that these websites are appropriate for children. However, because of the nature of the Internet, it is impossible to guarantee that these sites will remain active indefinitely or that their contents will not be altered.

INDEX